YOUR KNOWLEDGE HAS VALUE

Richards Macdonald

Conflict Management Process. The Case of the Poisoned Chalice

GRIN Verlag

Bibliografische Information der Deutschen Nationalbibliothek:

Die Deutsche Bibliothek verzeichnet diese Publikation in der Deutschen National-
bibliografie; detaillierte bibliografische Daten sind im Internet über http://dnb.d-
nb.de/ abrufbar.

Imprint:

Copyright © 2012 GRIN Verlag GmbH
Druck und Bindung: Books on Demand GmbH, Norderstedt Germany
ISBN: 978-3-656-45827-2

This book at GRIN:

http://www.grin.com/en/e-book/215741/conflict-management-process-the-case-of-
the-poisoned-chalice

GRIN - Your knowledge has value

Der GRIN Verlag publiziert seit 1998 wissenschaftliche Arbeiten von Studenten, Hochschullehrern und anderen Akademikern als eBook und gedrucktes Buch. Die Verlagswebsite www.grin.com ist die ideale Plattform zur Veröffentlichung von Hausarbeiten, Abschlussarbeiten, wissenschaftlichen Aufsätzen, Dissertationen und Fachbüchern.

Visit us on the internet:

http://www.grin.com/

http://www.facebook.com/grincom

http://www.twitter.com/grin_com

Executive Summary

Constant organizational changes inevitably lead to interpersonal and group conflicts within organizations. In order to mitigate the negative consequences of unresolved conflict, the conflict management process must be carefully managed. The intervention strategy employed to resolve the conflict depends upon the particular circumstances surrounding the particular case.

The conflict management process should begin with a careful diagnosis of the problem and measurement of the severity, extent and causes of the conflict. This should be followed by the implementation of the appropriate strategy which should involve some level of learning evidenced by new behaviours, and finally the process should be evaluated and the feedback examined to determine its effectiveness. Communication, management involvement, style and control, as well as the use of effective change management strategies, are essential elements of a successful conflict management process. Effective conflict management processes will shape and positively impact the culture of the organization.

If time pressure affects the conflict management process, it must be firmly controlled by the manager. Any previous failed attempts at conflict resolution by the manager should be corrected by engaging an external third party specialist to add objectivity and novelty to the situation. Change management strategies are necessary for lasting conflict management change and a transformational management style should be applied.

In cases where there is interpersonal and group conflict, the following recommendations should be considered:

- The Manager should take control of the process and carry out a comprehensive diagnosis of the conflict
- Use intervention by engaging a qualified Conflict Specialist for an initial 7 day period to facilitate communication, implement training and guide in behavioural change techniques
- The Manager should consider adopting a transformational leadership style and be prepared to lead the conflict management process as well as any change management process

Table of Contents

1.0   Introduction

Conflict is present in every organisation at one level or the other. Unresolved conflicts in the workplace tend to have negative consequences that impact on productivity, job satisfaction and interpersonal relationships (Carter & Byrnes, 2006).

1.1   Background Information

Joseph, the new Manager assigned to lead a taskforce of two teams, is faced with a challenge involving conflict between both teams; conflict between both teams and the other support departments; and the apparent undermining of his authority by his boss who tried to resolve the issue himself. Unknown to him until recently, this newly acquired, 5 month old taskforce, has had on going, unresolved conflicts arising out of team perceptions of the other team's superiority or inferiority and also due to fear-induced, antagonistic behaviour from the support departments. Because of the conflict and its negative impact on productivity, there is the possibility that the project will not be completed on time and that Joseph will be held responsible for the taskforce not meeting the project objectives.

1.2   Aims

The purpose of this report is to explore the conflict management process and to determine the conflict resolution approach that will best satisfy all parties involved in the most efficient, and effective manner, and in the shortest possible period of time given the deadline constraints.

1.3   Scope

This report will examine the various approaches to the conflict resolution management process at the workplace as well as give commentary on how successfully each approach has been applied in various situations in the past. The research was conducted using secondary data from a wide selection of scholarly sources.

2.0   Literature Analysis

The literature analysis involves a review of 3 scholarly articles which address how communication considerations, time pressure and group settings affect conflict management strategy and process. The articles each appear in academic journals spanning the period 2009 to 2010 and bear relevance to the determination of how conflicts should be handled in the modern organisation.

2.1   Fighting Futility: Tools for Mediation Success by Bultena, Ramser and Tilker (2010)

Conflict can be solved using a variety of methods. Although arbitration is commonly practised as an approach to conflict resolution, it is costly and usually results with one party being the winner and one party being the loser. In the workplace setting,
conflict is more effectively resolved when both parties feel satisfied that the solution is balanced and beneficial for each side. One approach to conflict resolution that has been growing in popularity and has resulted in numerous cases of successful conflict resolution is mediation (Bultena, Ramser and Tilker, 2010). Mediation involves the use of an objective third party who can facilitate constructive communication.

2.2   What Corporations need to know about how to install an Integrated   Conflict Management System by Cohen (2009)

In this article, the author recommends what is referred to as an Integrated Conflict Management System (ICMS) that has the objective of shaping the conflict management culture of the organisation. In this system, conflict resolution is dealt with by engaging an outsourced conflict management practitioner who focuses on improving communication between conflicting parties as a method of resolving conflict. The conflict expert encourages the disputants involved to view conflicts from novel perspectives and assists them by proposing options for dealing with the conflicts (Cohen, 2009). Alternately, mediation or peer review may be used to seek to address the issues by integrating different groups or individuals into the conflict resolution process.

2.3   Managing Intractable Identity Conflicts by Fiol, Pratt & O'Connor   (2009)

This piece endorses a conflict resolution process that incorporates several different phases in which parties are encouraged to change perceptions of their own identities in an effort to

foster group agreement. The authors claim that "when identities are implicated in a conflict, the conflict tends to escalate, encompassing an ever-widening number of issues" (Fiol, Pratt & O'Connor, 2009, p. 32). Conventional methods of resolving conflict such as mediation are described as ineffective in handling group conflicts in which identities are undermined or criticised.

3.0   The Conflict Management Process

Organizational changes are inevitable. However, the systems that are needed to assist employees to adjust to changes such as new job requirements, are either ineffective or non-existent (Zikiv, Marinovic & Trandafilovic, 2012). This situation usually leads to conflict as employees try to adjust to new situations. It is important that conflict management strategies be implemented to prevent the negative consequences of unresolved conflict including decreased productivity, frustration, job turnover and even violence.

Conflict management is a process that must start with a careful diagnosis of the conflict which would include measurement of the severity and scope of the conflict and the underlying reasons for it. This is followed by the application of appropriate intervention strategies which is dependent upon the particular circumstances of the case. During the process, some amount of learning should take place, which should impact on the behaviours of involved parties. Finally feedback is obtained, whether formally or informally, which determines whether further diagnosis and retracing of the entire process is necessary (Rahim, 2001).

The case involves a range of issues that must be addressed if the conflict is to be resolved effectively, fairly and efficiently. The sources of the conflict include poor communication, and fear-induced, antagonistic group behaviours as a result of the establishment of the two (2) different taskforce teams. The conflict has escalated because of conflict avoidance by the previous manager and the undermining of the authority of the current manager who has only recently been made aware of the on-going, unresolved conflict between the various groups. A diagnosis of the situation brings to light that there are at least two (2) levels of conflict to be tackled. These are interpersonal conflict between the manager and his boss, and between the Manager and individuals in all groups; as well as intergroup conflict among the two (2) taskforce groups and the support department.

The intervention aspect of the conflict management process will address the issues of communication, interpersonal and group conflict and the appropriate conflict management

strategies that need to be applied for the resolution of this particular case.

3.1   Communication

The strained relationships in the case are partially the result of the condescending comments and attitudes made by each group towards the other, the lack of communication between the groups and the deliberate withholding of pertinent information from the Manager (by his boss) regarding the on-going group conflict.

The importance of effective communication in the workplace cannot be over- emphasised. It has a significant bearing on interpersonal relationships, including management – employee relations, peer to peer interactions and relationships with parties external to the organisation. Job-satisfaction and productivity are also affected by the quality of communication in the work setting.

Conflicts often result from ineffective communication practices due to territorial behaviour or lack of collaboration and information exchange among individuals or groups (Cohen, 2009).

3.1.1   Managing the communication aspect of conflict

Helie (2001) believes that it is important that communication in the conflict resolution process be managed effectively through the timely scheduling of group meetings and discussions. Face to face communication is preferred to less personal methods such as using emails and conference calls when dealing with emotional and sensitive issues that arise out of conflicts in the workplace. Lack of interaction between in-groups and out-groups fosters prejudices and negative attitudes that may eventually become rooted. This means that there must be communication at the interpersonal level as well as between the groups involved.

Communication issues in conflict resolution must be tackled with the aim of transforming the organizational culture to facilitate on going, amicable and effective communication among individuals and groups within the organisation (Cohen, 2009). This may be achieved using intervention measures such as engaging a conflict specialist who is skilled at facilitating communication between conflicting groups and who acts as the catalyst for improving the conflict management culture of the organization (Cohen, 2009). In this particular case, engaging a third party might prove to be the better alternative to manager intervention since group members may have lost confidence in the manager's ability to effectively deal with the conflict. This lack of confidence could be as a result of the undermining of his authority by his boss as well as his inability to resolve the conflict effectively so far. However, the

manager must also be engaged in the process and his concerns must also be taken into consideration by the conflict specialist. It should be a learning experience for the manager and an enabling process for both himself and his subordinates so that conflicts can be effectively handled in the future.

3.2   Conflict among Groups

People naturally desire to be accepted as part of a group and to be identified as a worthy and valuable member of that group. Fiol, Pratt and O'Connor believe that "...many conflicts are characterized by tensions stemming from differences in how groups fundamentally define themselves and from threats to those self-definitions" (2009, p. 32). The two (2) taskforce groups in this case each see themselves as superior to the other group in some way or the other, and they also believe that they are superior to the members of the support departments. In-group esteem is built when out-groups are viewed in a negative light, as less capable and less acceptable. This process satisfies the desire of the individual for a positive self-image; and closeness within the in-group is fortified (Cuhadar & Dayton, 2011).

In managing conflict between and among groups, it must be established whether the conflict arose as a result of the formation of the groups or whether the conflict is a result of informal groups formed on the basis of identity or commonality. In other words, it needs to be clear whether the conflict has arisen as a result of change or has it just been escalated as a result of change. In any case, change has occurred. Change management becomes important in this regard as the culture of the organization must encourage appropriate change management strategies since change is inevitable in every organization.

It is a reasonable assumption that in this case, conflict has occurred as a result of both scenarios. Informal groups could have been established as a result of age group similarities or job function similarities within the organization. Employees identify themselves with other employees within their own age group or with persons who carry out similar job functions in the work setting. This is one of the bases for forming in-groups and out-groups. With the formation of the two (2) taskforce groups, the attractiveness of group identity is enhanced and becomes an avenue for positive self-image perceptions with each group viewing themselves as more competent, more knowledgeable or more capable of handling assigned tasks.

3.2.1 Management of Group Conflict

One approach to managing group conflicts is to bring the groups together to form one large group focused on accomplishing a particular task. It is believed that doing this might encourage increased understanding and appreciation of each other and therefore foster harmonious relations (Fiol et al, 2009). However, this approach has not always resulted in the desired resolution of the conflict and has in fact made the conflict worse in some cases. When the US healthcare authorities attempted to integrate physicians with hospitals, the outcome was a drop in productivity and resentment of the system by the physicians involved (Fiol et al, 2009). Van Kleef, Steinel and Horman (2013) believe that negotiation is the most constructive way of resolving group conflict. This negotiation would involve a negotiator who would facilitate dialogue between the groups with a view to arriving at an acceptable agreement. The outcome is highly dependent on the skill of negotiator in reaching a consensus that is acceptable to all parties involved. This approach is similar to the manager- led intervention approach touted by Elangovan (1998) in that the negotiator is normally an internal person just as the manager is an internal party to the process. What is essential is that group discussion is facilitated and encouraged so that the various issues can be appropriately handled.

Transformational leadership is necessary for resolving conflict and this involves influencing employees to reframe their thoughts and perceptions and to find new and creative ways of thinking and solving problems (Rahim, 2001). Joseph must become a transformational leader if the conflict issues are to be handled successfully.

3.3   Interpersonal Conflicts

As the name implies interpersonal conflict is conflict between individuals as opposed to conflicts between or among groups. Conflicts normally arise as a result of perceived deprivation or disadvantage on the part of the perceiver and the perception that the other party has an advantage or has 'won'.

3.3.1   Management of Interpersonal Conflicts

Similar to group conflicts, the management of the process must begin with diagnosis to detect the causes of the conflict and to learn how individuals handle conflict situations and whether their behaviour is conducive to the effective resolution of the conflict (Rahim, 2001). Individuals handle interpersonal conflict according to who the conflict involves; whether it

involves superiors, peers or subordinates. The most popular methods of interpersonal conflict management are collaboration and behaviour modification (Zikiv, Marinovi and Trandafilovic, 2012).

4.0   Conclusion

In order to ensure that the objectives of the taskforce, and ultimately the organisation, are met, it is important that all levels of conflict in the organization and the conflict management process be managed effectively. The two (2) most relevant levels of conflict in this case are interpersonal and group conflict. The chosen style of conflict management will depend on the findings of the initial and subsequent diagnoses. Because change is inevitable, the organization must be trained in change management strategies and the leaders must be prepared to lead and facilitate the process and to apply transformational leadership techniques. The conflict management process must be used to shape the organization's culture to a culture that handles change well and that is equipped with effective conflict management techniques.

5.0   Recommendations

Based on an analysis of the case, the following steps are recommended for the effective management of the conflict process.

- Using appropriate techniques, the manager should undertake a comprehensive diagnosis of the causes of the conflict and the severity of the situation
- Use intervention by engaging a qualified conflict specialist for an initial 7 day period, who can facilitate dialogue and candid communication, train the managers and the teams in behaviour management, and bring an objective perspective to the situation
- Because of time pressure, the process must be fully controlled by the manager and if this is effective the outcome will be 'controlled" by the individuals involved
- In the short to medium term, the Manager must adopt a transformational leadership style and be prepared to learn and apply effective change management strategies in the organization to facilitate a culture that is adaptive to change.

5.1   Financial Analysis

Financial resources are needed to fund the conflict management process. The aim is to implement a strategy that will have long lasting positive effects upon the organization. Funds are needed for the purchase of training material for staff, and the contraction of the conflict specialist. The training specialist will be engaged for a period of 7 days initially to give the task force project a jump start back on track. This will cost approximately $3000 per day for 7 days. The specialist will use his/her own equipment to undertake the task.

Financial Input

Conflict specialist @ $3,000.00 daily for 7 days	$21,000.00
Training materials	$ 2,000.00
Miscellaneous costs	$ 1,000.00

TOTAL COSTS   **$24,000.00**

5.2   Implementation Plan (Figure 1)

Activity	Start Date	Duration (days)	Finish Date
Interviewing of staff by Specialist	22-Apr-13	3	24-Apr-13
Present findings to Manager	25-Apr-13	1	25-Apr-13
Interviewing & Observation (by Specialist)	26-Apr-13	3	30-Apr-13
Program design (Specialist & Manager)	30-Apr-13	1	01-May-13
Training of Manager	02-May-13	1	02-May-03
Training of Staff	02-May-13	7	12-May-13
Evaluation & Feedback	22-Apr-13	16	14-May-13

The process will involve all staff including managers as well as the Conflict Resolution Specialist. The process will last approximately 16 days in the first instance.

References

Alessandra, A.J., Hunsaker, P.L. (2006). *Resolving conflict: eReport.* Electronic & Database Pub.

Bultena, C., Ramser, C., & Tilker, K. (2010). Fighting futility: Tools for mediation success. *Southern Journal of Business & Ethics, 2,* 64-73.

Carter, G., & Brynes, J.F. (2006). Chapter 1: Conflict in organizations. In, *How to manage Conflict in the organization, 2nd edition,* 1-31.

Cohen, J. (2009). What organizations need to know about how to install an integrated conflict Management system. *Alternatives to the High Cost of Litigation (1549 – 4373), 27*(6), 99-102. doi:10.1002/alt.20283

Cuhadar, E., & Dayton, B. (2011). The social psychology of identity and inter-group conflict: From theory to practice. *International Studies Perspectives, 12*(3), 273-293. doi:10.1111/j.1528-3585.2011.00433.x

Elangovan, A.R. (1998). Managerial intervention in organizational disputes: Testing a Prescriptive model to strategy selection. *International Journal of Conflict Management, 9*(4), 301-335.

Fiol, C., Pratt, M.G., & O'Connor, E.J. (2009). Managing intractable identity conflicts. *Academy Of Management Review, 34*(1), 32-55. doi:10.5465/AMR.2009.35713276

Helie, J. (2001). Using your communications options wisely: A multi-tool approach to conflict Resolution communication methods. *Journal of Alternative Dispute Resolution in Employment, 3*(1), 11-13.

Rahim, M. (2001). *Managing conflict in organizations.* Quorum Books.

Van Kleef, G.A, Steinel, W., & Horman, A.C. (2013). On being peripheral and paying attention: Prototypicality and information processing in intergroup conflict. *Journal of Applied Psychology, 98*(1), 63-79. doi:10.1037/a0030988

Zivik, S., Marinovic, A., & Trandafilovic, I. (2012). Promotion of conflict management Strategies in terms of modern business. *Megatrend Review, 9*(1), 201-221.